A Partnership

between the

United States

and Canada

Conserving
Borderline
Species

Contents

U.S.-Canada Framework for Cooperation

In April 1997, the U.S. and Canadian governments signed a Framework to cooperate in identifying and recovering shared species at risk. The official title is the "Framework for Cooperation between the U.S. Department of the Interior and Environment Canada in the Protection and Recovery of Wild Species at Risk." The goal of the Framework is to prevent populations of wild species shared by the United States and Canada from becoming extinct as a consequence of human activity, through the conservation of wildlife populations and the ecosystems on which they depend (p. 25).

Conserving Borderline Species:

A Partnership between the United States and Canada

INTRODUCTION

Wild species know no borders. Many inhabit ecological regions that stretch across political boundaries. Canada and the United States share several ecological regions – forests, mountain ranges, the coastal plains, the Great Plains, the Great Lakes, and the Arctic tundra. A great number of wild species, from western prairie fringed orchids to grizzly bears, occur in both countries, or migrate between them. Some of these species are also on the border of extinction and require urgent assistance. To get them this help, the two countries have signed a Framework to protect shared species at risk (p. 25).

The U.S. lists those species determined by the U.S. Fish and Wildlife Service and the National Marine Fisheries Service to be threatened or endangered under the Endangered Species Act. In the United States, 33 animal and plant species on this list also occur in Canada (p. 22-23).[1]

The Canadian list includes those species determined to be nationally at risk by the Committee on the Status of Endangered Wildlife in Canada (COSEWIC), an independent scientific body with representatives from Federal, Provincial, Territorial, and private agencies as well as independent experts. In Canada, 125 animal and plant species on this list are also found in the United States (p. 22-23).[1]

Joint U.S.-Canada conservation efforts are already underway. The 10 examples profiled on the following pages illustrate ways that binational efforts can improve a species' chance of survival and recovery. American and Canadian biologists share research, coordinate habitat protection, assist one another with on-the-ground species protection activities, and conduct joint reintroduction efforts.

For example, on the Pacific coast, experts from British Columbia, California, Oregon, and Washington are developing a survey protocol to locate the habitat of the secretive marbled murrelet. On the Great Plains of Manitoba, Minnesota, and North Dakota, experts are exchanging methods of securing voluntary management agreements with landowners in areas inhabited by the western prairie fringed orchid. In the Great Lakes area, scientists are conducting public consultations they hope will help recover the Lake Erie water snake. On the Atlantic coast, biologists coordinate a periodic exchange of experts to help enhance piping plover habitat.

Biologists are also reintroducing wild species to former habitats. Since the late 1960s, experts in the United States and Canada have bred whooping cranes in captivity and have reintroduced them to the wild, preventing the species' extinction. In the early 1980s, the United States started sending swift foxes to Canada to help re-establish a wild population in Alberta and Saskatchewan. In the late 1980s, Canada sent woodland caribou to the United States to augment a remnant herd in the Selkirk Mountains of Idaho and Washington. Canada also sent grizzly bears to Montana to augment the population in the Cabinet Mountains. In Ontario's Carolinian forest region, wildlife biologists are researching ways to reintroduce the Karner blue butterfly into the wild using breeding stock from Ohio. Canadian scientists are also breeding black-footed ferrets in captivity for reintroduction into western U.S. States.

The U.S. Fish and Wildlife Service and the Canadian Wildlife Service are responsible for implementing the Framework. Representatives from both agencies meet periodically to plan strategies for protecting shared species. Biologists have compiled lists of species of mutual concern to determine which ones are a priority for cooperative efforts. Hopefully, this agreement will strengthen recovery efforts for our borderline species.

---

[1] Since the U.S. Fish and Wildlife Service and the Canadian Wildlife Service have varying jurisdictions, the Framework does not currently consider issues involving marine mammals, fish, or sea turtles.

Black-footed Ferret
(Mustela nigripes)

STATUS

Canada (COSEWIC): Extirpated

U.S. (USFWS): Endangered; Experimental populations (specific portions of Arizona, Colorado, Montana, South Dakota, Utah, and Wyoming)

U.S. Fish and
Wildlife Service

DESCRIPTION

The black-footed ferret is North America's only native ferret species. It is about the size of a mink, reaching nearly 60 centimeters (2 feet) in total length and weighing up to 1.1 kilograms (2.5 pounds). It is buff colored with black legs and feet, a black-tipped tail, and a white face with a dark band across the eyes which forms a distinctive mask. It has short, rounded ears and large black eyes.

ECOLOGY

Black-footed ferrets prey primarily on prairie dogs and use prairie dog burrows for shelter and raising young. In fact, the ferret's historical range closely coincides with that of three prairie dog species. Ferrets breed in the spring, April to May, with a gestation period of about 42 days. Each female produces a litter of three or four kits on average. They don't mate for life, and the male plays no role in rearing. Kits begin to disperse at about four to five months of age.

CAUSES OF DECLINE

The black-footed ferret's known historical range once extended from the Canadian Prairie Provinces of Alberta and Saskatchewan to the southwestern United States, including twelve States: Arizona, Colorado, Kansas, Montana, Nebraska, New Mexico, North Dakota, Oklahoma, South Dakota, Texas, Utah, and Wyoming. Biologists can't be sure of the ferret's historical range abundance due to its nocturnal and secretive habits. In the last century, agricultural cultivation greatly reduced the ferret's prairie habitat. In addition, widespread prairie dog poisoning and sylvatic plague have drastically reduced prairie dog populations throughout North America, nearly exterminating the ferret. The absence of large, healthy prairie dog habitats remains the central threat to ferrets today.

RESEARCH AND RECOVERY

Canadian and U.S. scientists have been cooperating in black-footed ferret recovery since the early 1990s. In the late 1970s, ferrets were thought to be extinct. But in 1981, researchers discovered a small population near Meeteetse, Wyoming. By 1985, the Meeteetse population began to crash from diseases. To salvage the species, scientists captured all ferrets between 1985 and 1987 and moved them to a captive-breeding center at the Wyoming Game and Fish Department's Sybille Research Facility (now known as the U.S. Fish and Wildlife Service's National Black-footed Ferret Conservation Center). By 1988, biologists had succeeded in breeding and rearing kits in captivity, and began to expand the captive population to other breeding facilities. In 1991, they began reintroducing ferrets into the wild in the Shirley Basin of Wyoming. However, because of sylvatic plague in prairie dog populations, release efforts were suspended in Wyoming in 1995. Reintroduction projects were initiated in Montana and South Dakota in 1994, in Arizona in 1996, in Colorado and Utah in 1999, and at a second site in north-central South Dakota in 2000.

To date, only one potential self-sustaining population of ferrets has been established in the wild. In the Conata Basin/Badlands area of South Dakota, more than 60 wild-born litters and 150 kits were documented during the summer of 2000. Moderate success has also been achieved at a reintroduction area on the U.L. Bend National Wildlife Refuge in Montana where 16 litters and 43 kits were observed during the summer of 2000. Although Canadian scientists wish to reintroduce the ferret to the wilds of Alberta and Saskatchewan, black-tailed prairie dog numbers are currently insufficient to support a ferret population. No wild ferrets are known to exist today outside of the reintroduction areas.

In 1992, the Metro Toronto Zoo launched a black-footed ferret captive-breeding program. Since then, the zoo has sent captive-bred ferrets to reintroduction programs in three States. Wildlife biologists and zoo staff from Canada and the United States are cooperating to develop and refine captive-rearing methods to increase overall black-footed ferret production. The Metro Toronto Zoo has conducted valuable research in areas of reproduction, animal behavior, and ferret nutrition. A ferret diet devised at the zoo has become the standard diet used at the U.S. Fish and Wildlife Service's National Black-footed Ferret Conservation Center. In addition to the National Black-footed Ferret Conservation Center and the Metro Toronto Zoo, four zoos in the United States currently house and breed black-footed ferrets. The captive population now numbers 400 animals in six separately maintained locations.

Black-footed Ferret
Historical Range
● Reintroduction Sites (1991–2000)

In September of 2000, the Metro Toronto Zoo hosted the annual Black-footed Ferret Species Survival Plan meeting, which involves Canadian and U.S. scientists working to re-establish the ferret. Experts in captive production of ferrets attended the meeting to help direct future management and recovery efforts for the species, and to select genetic pairings for future ferret breeding.

Swift Fox

(Vulpes velox)

STATUS

Canada (COSEWIC): Endangered

U.S. (USFWS): Endangered (Canadian population of V. velox hebes*)*

DESCRIPTION

The swift fox is the smallest member of the North American wild dog family. Named for its quickness, a swift fox is only the size of a house cat but can keep pace with a jackrabbit at speeds of over 60 kilometers (37 miles) per hour. The swift fox is buffy-yellow, with fur that grows thicker toward the end of summer. It has a black tip on its bushy tail, and large, pointed ears, with characteristic black shading on its muzzle.

Lu Carbyn

ECOLOGY

Swift foxes are mainly nocturnal. During the day they usually remain in the vicinity of the den. They often live in pairs, although they may not mate for life. Breeding occurs during January and February, and the average spring litter consists of four or five pups. Swift foxes eat mostly mice, cottontail rabbits, and carrion, although they will also feed on other small mammals, birds, insects, reptiles, and amphibians. Swift foxes prefer open, sparsely vegetated short-grass and mixed-grass prairie, where they have a good view and can move about easily.

CAUSES OF DECLINE

The swift fox once ranged from the Canadian Prairies to Texas, but suffered a severe decline beginning in the early 1900s. It disappeared from Canada, but remains in 9 of 10 States where it was historically found, most commonly in Colorado, Kansas, and Wyoming. A thorough review by the Northern Prairie Wildlife Research Center (North Dakota) of the swift fox's historical range and current distribution indicates it still occurs throughout approximately 40 percent of its historical range. Hunting, loss of habitat, accidental trapping and poisoning during predator control programs, and harsh winters and droughts all contributed to the disappearance of the swift fox from Canada. The conversion of native prairie grasslands to farmland has reduced the quantity and quality of available swift fox habitat. Current threats include ongoing cultivation and development on the prairie and competition from coyotes for food and living space.

Canadian and U.S. experts have cooperated closely in swift fox reintroduction efforts in Canada. Since 1973, a total of 151 wild foxes have been captured in Colorado, South Dakota, and Wyoming. Some of these foxes were sent to Canadian captive-breeding facilities, while many others were released directly into the Canadian wild. Since 1983, more than 800 captive-raised swift foxes were released in Alberta and Saskatchewan. Most of these foxes were from captive colonies raised in facilities at Cochrane, Alberta, and Moose Jaw, Saskatchewan. Despite severe winter weather and predation by bobcats, coyotes, and eagles, many foxes survived and have begun reproducing. The latest population estimate (1996) is of 289 swift foxes in the wild in Canada, the majority on the Alberta/Saskatchewan border, plus a small population in adjacent areas of Montana.

In 1998, at the request of the Blackfeet Tribe, Canada and the United States began a cooperative reintroduction program of swift foxes on the Blackfeet Reservation in Montana. The Blackfeet Tribe invited Alberta's Cochrane Ecological Institute to help conduct the project. The Institute agreed to provide swift fox offspring from its captive colony, and participated in release planning, permitting, and academic liaison and research.

Two reintroductions took place, the first one in 1998 and a second one in 1999. Follow-up surveys indicated that the swift foxes released in 1998 were surviving and reproducing in the wild. Since 1998, Canadian scientists have cooperated with Montana to define the size and extent of the swift fox population that has spread from Canadian releases into the United States.

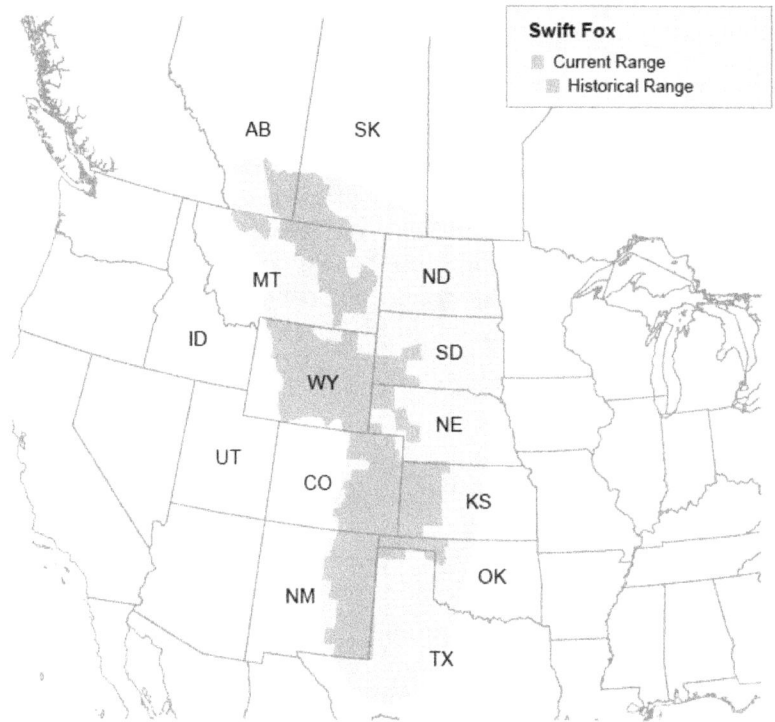

Woodland Caribou

(Rangifer tarandus caribou)

STATUS

Canada (COSEWIC): Endangered (Atlantic-Gaspésie population); Threatened (Boreal and Southern Mountain populations)

U.S. (USFWS): Endangered (Selkirk population)

DESCRIPTION

The woodland caribou is the largest caribou subspecies in North America. Its body is covered in long, thick hairs that are mostly brown in summer and nearly gray in winter. It has large feet with crescent-shaped, cloven hooves for walking in snow or swamps. A creamy white color is noticeable on the caribou's neck, mane, underbelly, and the underside of the tail. It also has a white shoulder stripe, and white patches just above each hoof. Woodland caribou grow antlers each year, and shed them in winter.

ECOLOGY

In Canada, woodland caribou herds generally remain in mature forest areas, often near marshes, bogs, lakes, and rivers. In mountainous environments, caribou inhabit subalpine and alpine habitats. In the United States, the Selkirk population inhabits high elevation ridges and mountainsides, descending in early winter to mature and old growth cedar/hemlock and spruce/fir stands which provide protection from the snow. In winter, caribou eat primarily ground and tree lichens. They also eat shrubs, grasses, and willows. Females usually begin reproducing at three years of age. The breeding season occurs in early- to mid-October. Pregnant females migrate to remote, secluded sites at high elevations or marshy areas to give birth. Calves, usually one per female, are born in late spring or early summer.

André Dumont

(Rangifer tarandus caribou)

CAUSES OF DECLINE

Woodland caribou declined in the 1800s and early 1900s, largely from over-hunting and predation. Today, most caribou herds are declining or remain stable at low numbers. Overall numbers have declined to less than 200,000 in Canada and the United States, including just under 50,000 in the boreal population that stretches from Alaska and British Columbia to Labrador. A few thousand occur in southern Alberta and British Columbia. A remnant population of just 35 caribou inhabits the Selkirk Mountains of southeastern British Columbia, northern Idaho, and northeastern Washington. Current threats include habitat degradation and fragmentation, predation by wolves, mountain lions, and bears, as well as human disturbance. In many parts of caribou range, habitat has been depleted, altered, or fragmented by logging practices, which reduce the amount of ground and tree lichens. Other threats include agriculture, oil and gas exploration, and mining. Forest fires have also contributed to habitat alteration.

RESEARCH AND RECOVERY

Since the late 1980s, the provincial government of British Columbia has cooperated with several U.S. agencies to bolster a remnant herd of woodland caribou in the southern Selkirk Mountains. The Province provided caribou for two separate augmentation projects conducted by the U.S. Fish and Wildlife Service, the U.S. Forest Service, and the States of Idaho and Washington. One occurred between 1987 and 1990, and the other between 1996 and 1998, totaling 103 caribou. Provincial officials participate in the U.S. Fish and Wildlife Service's woodland caribou recovery team and the International Mountain Caribou Technical Committee.

As part of the Selkirk Mountains project, wildlife biologists radio-collared all translocated animals and have monitored them since their release. Biologists also conducted annual aerial winter surveys to monitor the entire Selkirk Mountain population. The transplanted caribou experienced relatively high death rates. Since 1997, half of the caribou that existed in the herd prior to the translocation have also died. Although the cause of death is unknown in many cases, predation was a significant factor in known deaths. The population currently consists of 35 caribou, as compared to 25 to 30 in the mid-1980s. Scientists believe that this cooperative venture has temporarily prevented the Selkirk Mountain caribou population from becoming extirpated.

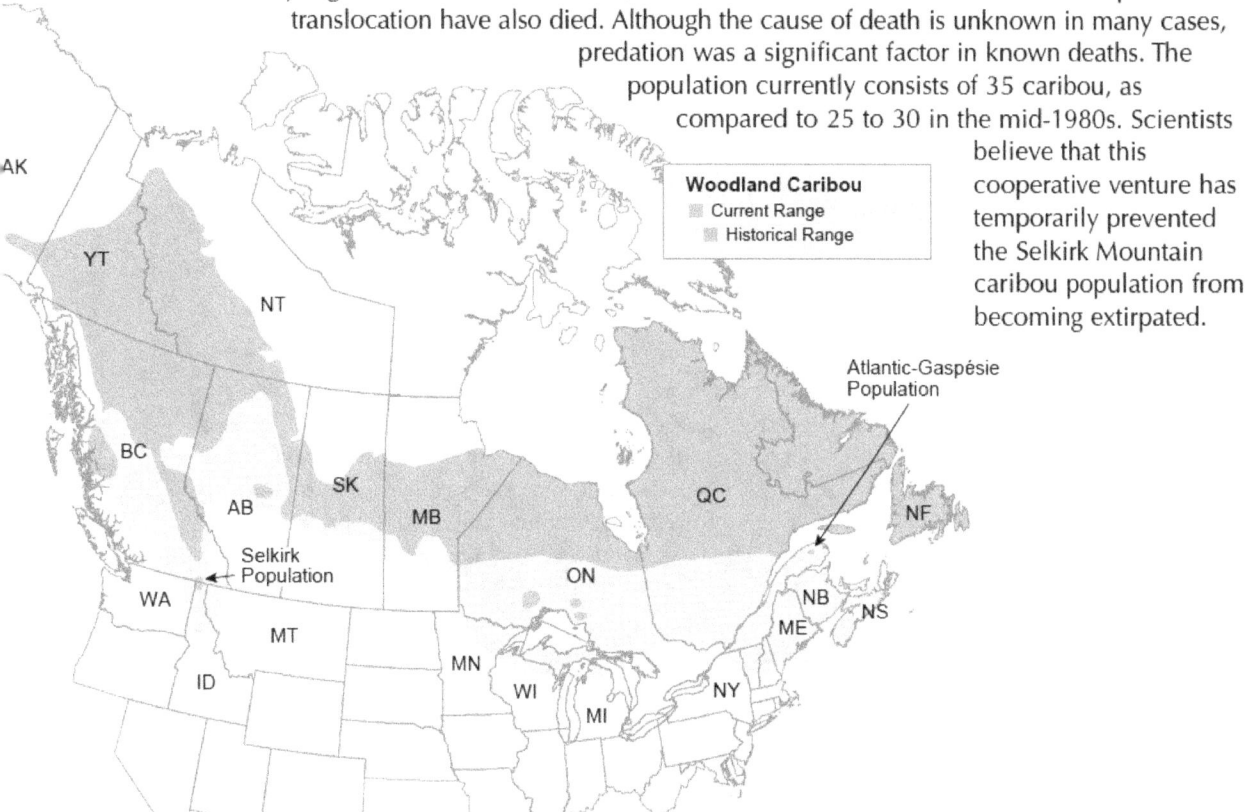

Woodland Caribou
Current Range
Historical Range

Atlantic-Gaspésie Population

Selkirk Population

Grizzly Bear

(Ursus arctos)

STATUS

Canada (COSEWIC): Extirpated (Prairie population); Special Concern

U.S. (USFWS): Threatened (Lower 48 States); Experimental populations (portions of Idaho and Montana)

DESCRIPTION

The grizzly bear is a solitary, smaller form of the brown bear. Larger than a black bear, the grizzly bear has a characteristic hump on its shoulders, a dished-in nose, and long fur that ranges in color from a creamy yellow to black, usually with some white-tipped hairs around the face and on the shoulders, creating a grizzled appearance. The thick winter underfur is rubbed off in the late spring.

Parks Canada/
Wayne Lynch

ECOLOGY

The grizzly bear has a large home range and many specific habitat requirements. It needs adequate spring, summer, and fall foods, appropriate sites to den, suitable protective cover, and isolation from human disturbance. Grizzly bears are omnivorous and feed on berries, salmon, plants, insects, and mammals ranging in size from ground squirrels to moose calves. They might even feed on a beached whale or other carrion. Bears are most active in the evening and early morning hours. Breeding occurs in June and July. Cubs, usually two per litter, are born in the den in January and February. In late autumn, grizzly bears excavate a hole or seek the shelter of a natural cavity for their winter dens, hibernating until early spring.

CAUSES OF DECLINE

The grizzly bear's range once extended across the western half of North America from Alaska to Mexico. Its range still spans the Provinces of Alberta and British Columbia and the States of Idaho, Montana, Washington, and Wyoming. The grizzly bear also inhabits Alaska and Canada's three northern Territories: the Northwest Territories, Nunavut, and the Yukon. The total Canadian population is estimated at about 22,000 bears. Humans are responsible for the grizzly bear's historical decline, through unregulated hunting and habitat degradation. Today, bear hunting is regulated in Canada and prohibited in the Lower 48 States. Nevertheless, the grizzly continues to face the risk of habitat disturbance, including habitat loss, habitat fragmentation, increased human disturbance, and high road density.

RESEARCH AND RECOVERY

Since the early 1980s, U.S. and Canadian wildlife experts have cooperated to coordinate grizzly bear recovery in Idaho, Montana, Washington, Wyoming, and southern portions of Alberta and British Columbia. To follow the bears' movements and other activities, scientists trap grizzly bears on both sides of the border, fit them with radio-collars, then monitor the radio signals by aircraft. Scientists have developed a computer model to predict possible grizzly bear habitat linkages. Experts in both countries are using the model's results to potentially maintain and re-establish connections between grizzly bear populations and habitats.

In the early 1990s, scientists augmented a small U.S. population by translocating four young female grizzly bears from British Columbia into the Cabinet Mountains of Montana. In 1995, the provincial government in British Columbia launched a Grizzly Bear Conservation Strategy which aims to maintain grizzly bear abundance throughout the Province. Under the strategy, the government created an independent committee consisting of Canadian and U.S. scientists to advise the B.C. Minister of the Environment on grizzly bear conservation.

In another joint effort, scientists from both countries participate on the Rocky Mountain Grizzly Bear Planning Committee, which coordinates data collection and management actions on grizzly bears in the Rocky Mountains from the north side of Jasper National Park in Alberta south to northwestern Montana.

In 1999, the British Columbia government launched recovery planning for specified habitat areas with threatened grizzly bear populations. As part of this initiative, scientists from Canada and the United States are drafting a recovery plan for the North Cascades grizzly population in British Columbia along the U.S. border, where few grizzly bears remain. The plan will address habitat protection, reduction of bear-human conflicts, improvement of public information and education, and research and monitoring of the North Cascades grizzly bears. Meanwhile, in the United States, biologists are completing a plan to re-establish a grizzly bear population in the largest block of wilderness in the U.S. Rocky Mountains. The reintroduced population will consist of a combination of bears from each country.

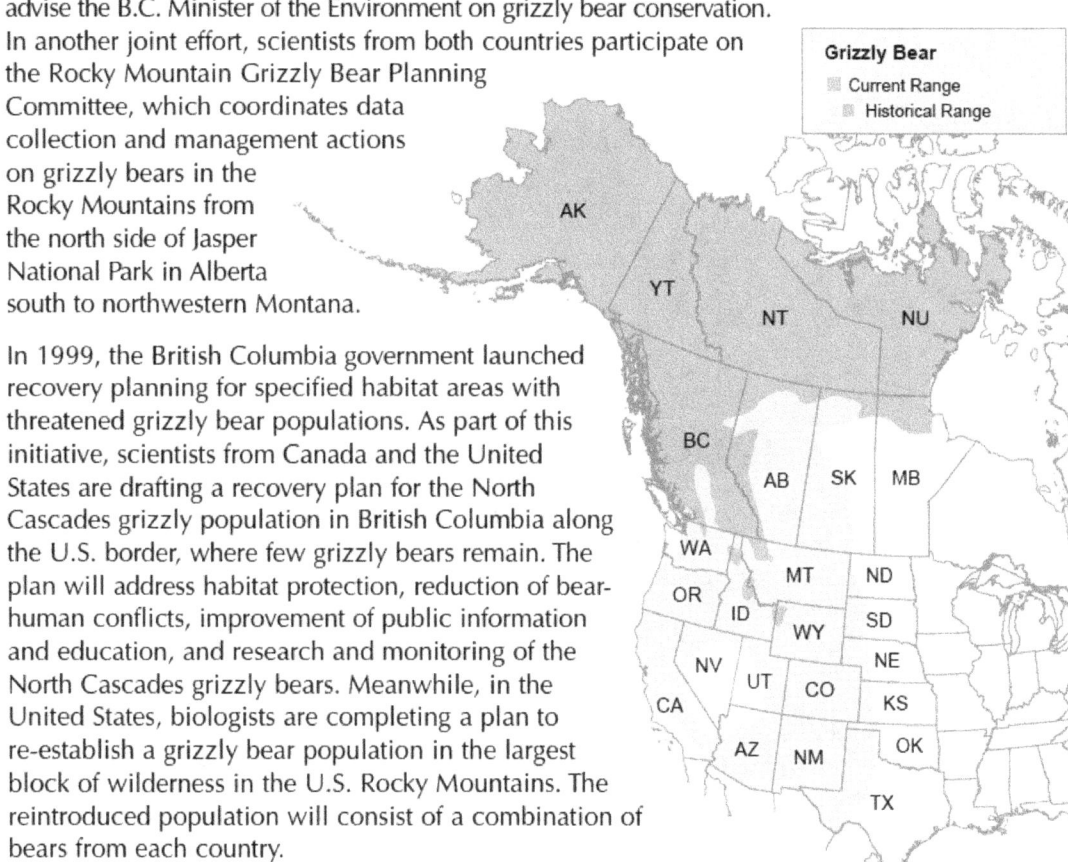

Grizzly Bear
Current Range
Historical Range

Whooping Crane

(Grus americana)

STATUS

Canada (COSEWIC): Endangered

U.S. (USFWS): Endangered; Experimental populations (Colorado, Florida, Idaho, New Mexico, Utah, and Wyoming)

Brian Johns

DESCRIPTION

Standing 1.5 meters (5 feet) tall, the whooping crane is the tallest bird in North America. Boasting a snowy white body and thin black legs, it has a long, pointed beak, a long neck, and a white and black head with a red crown. It has immense, black-tipped wings that allow it to glide with little effort and stay aloft for up to 10 hours at a time.

ECOLOGY

Whooping cranes migrate north from their wintering grounds in March and April. They breed in the boreal wetlands of Canada's Wood Buffalo National Park. The nest is usually a flat-topped mound of vegetation in shallow water. The female lays one clutch per year which usually consists of two eggs, but most often only one chick will fledge. Both adults incubate the eggs and raise the young. Whooping cranes feed on crustaceans, fish, small mammals, insects, roots, berries, and grain. They begin migrating south in early September.

CAUSES OF DECLINE

Historically, the whooping crane ranged from an area near the Arctic Circle south to central Mexico and from Utah east to the Atlantic coast. Having once numbered at least 10,000 birds, by the late 1800s the total global population had decreased to an estimated 1,500 individuals and continued to decrease. The decline was due to hunting, egg collection, and habitat disturbances such as conversion of wetlands for agriculture. By 1941, global whooping crane numbers had sunk to a low of 22 birds. Of these, 16 birds comprised a migratory flock that bred at Wood Buffalo National Park in Canada and wintered at the Aransas National Wildlife Refuge in southern Texas. A remnant population of six non-migratory whooping cranes existed in Louisiana, but by 1949 this population died out.

Human activities, such as poaching and development, continue to be chief threats to whooping cranes. Their migration corridor is undergoing continuous industrial development, causing incidents such as fatal collisions with power lines. During the breeding season, a drought or bad storm could destroy eggs and newly hatched chicks. On the wintering grounds, oil and chemical pollution in the bays along the Texas coast could destroy the remaining habitat, while a hurricane could wipe out the entire flock. In the winter of 2000/2001, there were approximately 180 birds in the Wood Buffalo-Aransas flock.

In the late 1940s, government agencies in Canada and the United States began actively sharing data and expertise to prevent the extinction of the whooping crane. In 1967, the Canadian Wildlife Service and the U.S. Fish and Wildlife Service launched a whooping crane captive-breeding program for release into the wild. Scientists transported eggs from Wood Buffalo National Park by air 3,453 kilometers (2,145 miles) to the Patuxent Wildlife Research Center in Laurel, Maryland. In 1989, a whooping crane breeding facility was established at the International Crane Foundation in Wisconsin.

Canadian biologists created a captive-breeding facility at the Calgary Zoo in 1993, the same year U.S. officials began establishing a non-migratory flock in Florida using cranes from the U.S. and Canadian facilities. In 1996, after 230 eggs had been collected, biologists discontinued egg collection for captive rearing. The flock in Florida numbers about 80 birds, but has yet to successfully raise young. In the spring of 2000, one pair hatched two eggs, the first whooping crane eggs to hatch in the wild in the United States in 60 years. One of the chicks died within two weeks. The parents raised the other to fledging age, before it fell prey to a bobcat.

Since 1990, the United States has helped Canadian scientists conduct aerial surveys on the cranes' reproductive success on the nesting grounds in Wood Buffalo National Park. In the spring of 2000, they discovered 50 nests, tying the record for the most ever found in one spring. In 1993, scientists began tracking sandhill crane migratory routes to identify their wintering areas and determine whether sandhill cranes could be used as guide birds for whooping cranes. Since 1993, scientists have been using ultralight aircraft to teach a specific migration route to surrogate sandhill cranes. Biologists also initiated studies into potential crane reintroduction habitat in Manitoba, Saskatchewan, and Wisconsin, hoping to eventually establish a new Wisconsin-Florida migratory flock of whooping cranes.

For 15 years, Canada and the United States have conducted formal joint recovery efforts. In 1985, the two countries signed a Memorandum of Understanding (MOU) to improve coordination and joint cooperation in whooping crane conservation. The document has been renewed in 1990 and 1995. The 1995 renewal confirmed a goal of increasing whooping crane numbers in the Wood Buffalo-Aransas flock to one thousand individuals (an objective first established in the species' 1994 U.S. recovery plan). Officials expect to renew the MOU in 2001. In 1996, Canada and the United States formed a joint Whooping Crane Recovery Team that meets once every year or two. The team consists of five members from each country. Whooping crane recovery plans in the two countries are currently being combined into a single plan.

Piping Plover

(Charadrius melodus)

STATUS

Canada (COSEWIC): Endangered

U.S. (USFWS): Endangered (Great Lakes population); Threatened (Atlantic Coast and Northern Great Plains populations)

DESCRIPTION

The piping plover is a small, stocky, sandy-colored bird with yellow-orange legs, and resembles a sandpiper. In summer, the plover develops breeding plumage with a black band across the forehead from eye to eye and a black ring around the base of its neck. In winter, these marks are absent (see photo). Like other plovers, it runs in short bursts. The bird derives its name from its call notes, plaintive bell-like whistles that are often heard before the bird is seen.

ECOLOGY

Piping plovers arrive on their breeding grounds during mid-March through mid-May and leave again by late August. They breed on the northern Great Plains, including the Canadian prairies, and along the Atlantic coast from Newfoundland to North Carolina. They also breed along the U.S. shores of the Great Lakes. They winter on the Atlantic and Gulf of Mexico coasts from North Carolina to Mexico, in the Bahamas, West Indies, and in Cuba. In 1996, there were nearly 6,000 breeding individuals throughout the plover's range, including 20 States, 9 Provinces, and the French islands of St-Pierre-Miquelon off Newfoundland's southern coast.

U.S. Fish and Wildlife Service

Piping plovers lay three to four eggs in shallow depressions lined with light-colored pebbles. The eggs are speckled with dark brown or black spots that make them scarcely distinguishable from the pebbles. Both partners incubate the eggs, which hatch within 26 to 28 days. Both sexes also tend to the chicks during feeding and resting, and continue to safeguard them until they can fly, at about 25 days.

CAUSES OF DECLINE

Historically, habitat loss and degradation due to coastal development were the major contributors to this species' decline. The plover is now threatened largely by predation. Gulls, crows, raccoons, and skunks (all predators that thrive around human development) prey on plover eggs and young. Another significant threat is from human recreation. Walking, jogging, and operating vehicles on beaches prevent plovers from feeding, flush them from roost sites, and destroy camouflaged eggs. Similar threats face the plover on its wintering grounds.

RESEARCH AND RECOVERY

Since 1988, Canadian and U.S. wildlife experts have shared information regularly about piping plover conservation strategies, such as beach guardian programs. Scientists exchange technical knowledge on banding, capture techniques, census methods and results, predator management, and all aspects of management of breeding and wintering populations. An International Piping Plover Coordination Group, comprised of Canadian and U.S. biologists, also facilitates information exchange and is coordinating recovery efforts.

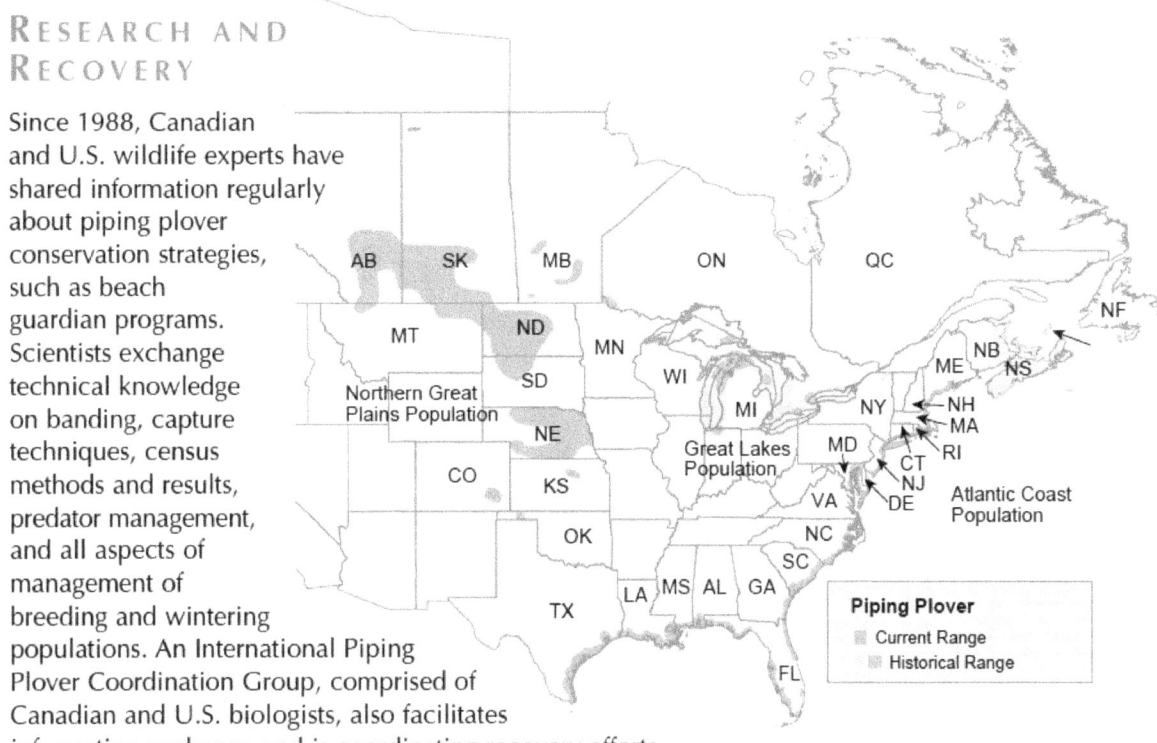

This exchange of information has led biologists in both countries to employ innovative recovery methods. In breeding areas, experts direct human traffic around the fragile nests on beaches and erect wire fencing around nests to keep predators out. On the Great Plains water bodies, such as the Missouri River in the United States and Lake Diefenbaker in Canada, officials try to maintain water levels conducive to plover nesting. The two countries also exchange biologists to assist with specific projects. The United States sent two biologists to Canada in the mid-1990s to help resolve problems with predator exclosures in Nova Scotia. In 1998, a Canadian biologist participated in a review of wintering habitat issues in Texas. In 1994, the United States sent four biologists to help census plovers in Atlantic Canada.

In 1991 and 1996, wildlife officials from each country participated in two international censuses of breeding and wintering plovers. These censuses gave the first global population counts for the plover. More than a thousand biologists and volunteers from several countries participated in the census, including many government agencies and conservation groups. The results indicated that the plover's status remains precarious due to its low population numbers, sparse distribution, continued threats to habitat, and low reproductive success throughout its range.

Marbled Murrelet

(Brachyramphus marmoratus)

STATUS

Canada (COSEWIC): Threatened

U.S. (USFWS): Threatened (California, Oregon, Washington)

DESCRIPTION

The marbled murrelet is a quail-sized bird with a plump body. It swims with its bill pointed upward, and flies in zigzags low over the water. Like most migratory birds, the marbled murrelet has different breeding and wintering plumages. The breeding plumage is dull brown on top, with "marbled" brown and white underparts. In winter, the bird is black with white on its throat, white shoulder patches, and white underparts. In autumn, the young resemble the adults in winter plumage, but the underparts have fine dusky bars.

John Deal

ECOLOGY

The marbled murrelet is an unusual seabird. It prefers to nest high in the well-hidden canopy of old-growth forests. By contrast, most seabirds nest in large colonies in burrows and crevices on offshore islands. In the northern part of its range, the murrelet nests in trees but also on the ground in treeless areas. Each May, adult marbled murrelets fly inland as far as 80 kilometers (50 miles) to nest. The birds are solitary nesters, and lay their single egg in a cup-shaped depression in thick mosses found on large branches. Both males and females incubate the egg in 24-hour shifts. While one incubates the egg, the other stays on the ocean, and flies back to the nest to feed the chick and change places with its mate. Once the egg hatches, they change places and feed the chick more frequently. The exchanges are most common in the early morning and in the evening. After the nesting season, marbled murrelets fish the coastal waters of the North Pacific throughout the fall. In more northern latitudes, they are usually forced farther out to sea in the winter by coastal ice formation and the limited availability of small fish.

CAUSES OF DECLINE

In the United States, the marbled murrelet occurs along the Pacific coast from the Canadian border to northern California, as well as in Alaska. In Canada, it is found off the coast of British Columbia and around coastal lakes. The estimated population is 301,000 in the United States and 50,000 to 60,000 in Canada. Major threats to the marbled murrelet are oil spills, their incidental catch in commercial fishery nets, and the destruction of habitat due to timber operations. Old-growth forest harvesting removes the bird's nesting habitat, while the toxic effects of leaked oil have directly killed thousands of marbled murrelets.

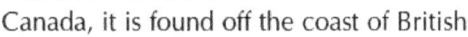

Marbled Murrelet
 Historical and Current Range

RESEARCH AND RECOVERY

Since the mid-1980s, Canadian and U.S. wildlife biologists have cooperated on marbled murrelet conservation and recovery issues. In 1972, scientists created an international organization called the Pacific Seabird Group to undertake seabird research and conservation. The group established a Marbled Murrelet Technical Committee in 1988 that includes Canadian and U.S. representatives. The committee meets annually to share information on recovery issues and the conservation status of marbled murrelets in the United States and Canada. The committee coordinates an ongoing effort to develop and update an inland survey protocol for marbled murrelets in British Columbia, California, Oregon, and Washington. Marbled murrelets are secretive and difficult to detect at inland forest stands, and a reliable survey technique is important for identifying nesting areas.

In Canada, scientists are also focusing recovery efforts on searching for murrelet nesting sites. Officials impose interim habitat protection measures in areas where nests are known to exist. Various forest companies on Vancouver Island have voluntarily deferred harvesting old-growth habitats used by marbled murrelets. As part of the U.S. and Canadian recovery efforts, biologists are emphasizing the need to reduce marbled murrelet mortality from net fisheries in the marine environment. The U.S. Fish and Wildlife Service and the Canadian Wildlife Service are collaborating to devise methods to assess the number of marbled murrelets caught in commercial fishing nets, and subsequently to reduce the incidental net entanglement of marbled murrelets.

(Brachyramphus marmoratus)

Lake Erie Water Snake

(Nerodia sipedon insularum)

STATUS

Canada (COSEWIC): Endangered

U.S. (USFWS): Threatened

Robert J. Willson

DESCRIPTION

The Lake Erie water snake is a non-venomous reptile that grows to almost 1 meter (3 feet) in length. The snake does not have fangs, but rather tiny teeth or ridges similar to those of some large trout. It usually retreats when approached by people. If threatened, however, the snake tends to flatten its head and body, and may strike out to give a pinching bite. In an effort to escape when captured, it might release a foul smell. The adult Lake Erie water snake is uniformly gray or has incomplete band patterns, plus dull body and shiny head scales. The Lake Erie water snake resembles the closely related northern water snake, but often lacks the body markings, or has only a pale version of those patterns.

ECOLOGY

During warm months, Lake Erie water snakes usually stay close to the shoreline, seeking the shelter of shrubs lining beaches or the trees along rocky shores. They feed on fish and amphibians in nearby waters up to 9 meters (30 feet) deep. The snakes congregate to breed. The offspring hatch from mid-August through September. The average clutch size is 23 young. During winter months, they move farther inland above the water and ice line. They hibernate in crevices of cliffs, rocky areas, tree root clusters, animal burrows, quarries, deserted cisterns and drainage tiles, old rock walls, or foundations.

CAUSES OF DECLINE

The Lake Erie water snake once inhabited 22 offshore islands and rock outcrops of western Lake Erie between the Ohio and Ontario mainland, and a portion of the Ontario mainland. It has disappeared from the Ontario mainland and several islands in both countries. It is now known primarily from only eight U.S. islands (Ballast, Gibraltar, Kelleys, Middle Bass, North Bass, Rattlesnake, South Bass, and Sugar) and four Canadian islands (East Sister, Hen, Middle, and Pelee). The snake inhabits the shoreline areas, nearshore waters, and nearby rock outcrops of these 12 islands.

The current estimate for the U.S. portion of the population ranges from 1,500 to 2,000 adults. The Canadian population is unknown. Persecution by humans is a major cause of the snake's decline and continues to be a chief threat. Loss of habitat from shoreline alteration and development over the past 60 years has also been a major cause of its decline. Other current threats include pesticides and oil spills.

Research and Recovery

Cross-border cooperation in the recovery of the Lake Erie water snake is a key objective for both Canada and the United States. In 1984, researchers assessed the population status, distribution, and habitat needs of the Lake Erie water snake in Ohio and Ontario waters. Since 1992, Canadian scientists have been working on a recovery plan with several long-term objectives, including developing liaisons with U.S. Federal agencies and the State of Ohio. In the United States, the U.S. Fish and Wildlife Service and Ohio Division of Wildlife are developing a Federal recovery plan and pursuing conservation plans on certain islands. Other key objectives under both plans will be to identify all suitable habitat types, and protect, enhance, monitor, and increase the population.

The U.S. portion of the population was reassessed in 1997 and 1998. Of five core islands most important to the snake, one is in Canada and four occur in the United States. On Pelee Island, Ontario, Provincial preserves at Fish Point and Lighthouse Point protect Lake Erie water snake habitat. In the United States, the U.S. Fish and Wildlife Service and the Ohio Division of Wildlife have conducted a public outreach program on the Lake Erie islands since 1994. The program encourages island residents and visitors to adopt a "live and let live" attitude toward snakes living among them. It includes a poster contest, an outdoor sign campaign, and personal contacts to inform island residents and visitors that Lake Erie water snakes are nonvenomous and pose little threat.

In the future, cooperating wildlife agencies expect public participation (for example, education, planning, project consultation) to play an important role in the Lake Erie water snake's recovery. Consultations might bring about additional habitat protection, habitat restoration, and modification of construction activity. Some day, beneficial shoreline projects could contain designs that utilize rock and vegetation to provide cover and forage areas for Lake Erie water snakes.

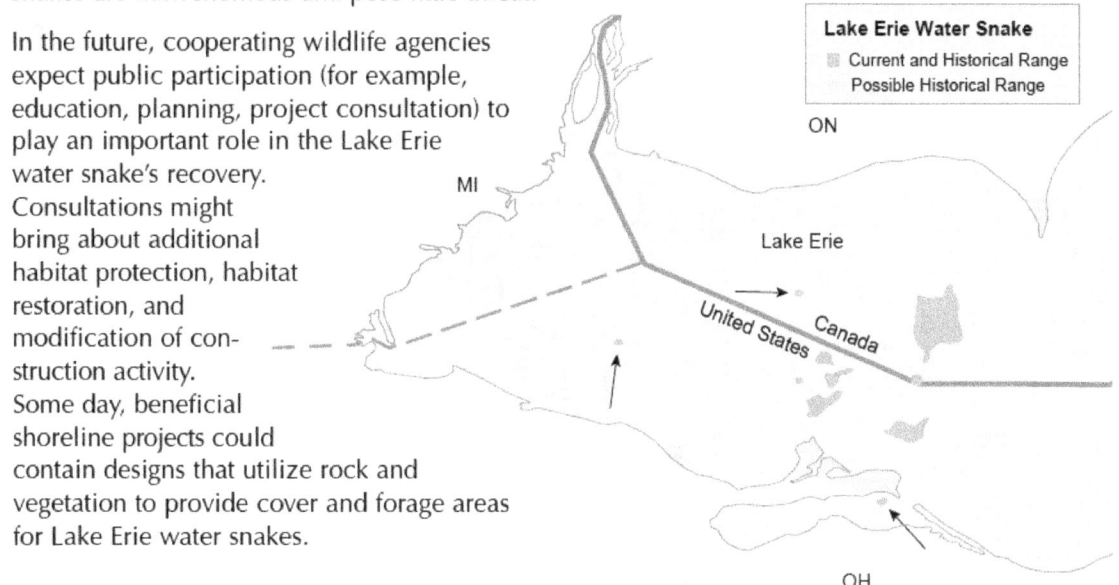

Lake Erie Water Snake
Current and Historical Range
Possible Historical Range

ON

MI

Lake Erie

United States   Canada

OH

Karner Blue Butterfly

(Lycaeides melissa samuelis)

STATUS

Canada (COSEWIC): Extirpated

U.S. (USFWS): Endangered

DESCRIPTION

The Karner blue butterfly is tiny, with a wingspan of just 2.5 centimeters (1 inch). The underside of both sexes is gray to fawn in color with orange crescents and metallic spots on the wings. The male has a silvery to dark blue topside with bold black margins near the edges of its wings. The female has a grayish brown to blue topside with irregular bands of orange crescents along the bottom back portion of both wings. The edges of its wings also have bold black margins. The outer edge of the butterfly's wings are lined with white scales called the fringe.

ECOLOGY

To survive, Karner blue butterfly larvae depend entirely on a single species of plant, the wild lupine *(Lupinus perennis)*. For food and reproduction the butterfly inhabits the same prairie and savannah habitats as wild lupines. It usually lays two batches of eggs each year, the first batch in July, on or near wild lupines. The emerging caterpillars feed on wild lupine leaves, and after becoming adult butterflies, lay their own eggs. By the end of August or early September all adult butterflies die. The second batch of eggs does not hatch until the following spring. Winter snows protect the eggs, which fall to the ground, from frost and dehydration. The Karner blue butterfly only occurs within the portion of the wild lupine range where long periods of winter snows occur.

Béla A. Nagy

CAUSES OF DECLINE

Karner blue butterflies once occurred in a nearly continuous narrow band across 10 States and the Province of Ontario. In the 20th century, the butterfly became extirpated in Ontario and nearly eliminated from at least six States. The butterfly declined due to conversion of prairie habitat for farming, land development for commercial and residential uses, and suppression of wild fires. Without fires, shrubs and trees invade the open savanna and barrens, shading out the grasses and herbaceous plants like wild lupine. Today, the butterfly is found in portions of Indiana, Michigan, Minnesota, New Hampshire, New York, and Wisconsin. Lack of habitat continues to be a major threat to the butterfly.

RESEARCH AND RECOVERY

Since the late 1980s, U.S. and Canadian wildlife experts have been exploring the feasibility of reintroducing Karner blue butterflies to their former Canadian habitat in Ontario. Under this initiative, butterflies from the United States would be used to start a captive-bred colony in Ontario, which in turn would be the source for the reintroduction into the wild. Ideally, the butterflies would be able to breed in the wild and establish self-sustaining populations. The Metro Toronto Zoo is developing a protocol for captive rearing of the butterflies. This research involves determining requirements, particularly food requirements, for raising butterflies in captivity in Canada. The zoo is using the tailed blue butterfly as a prototype, since it is a species with similar characteristics to the Karner blue butterfly.

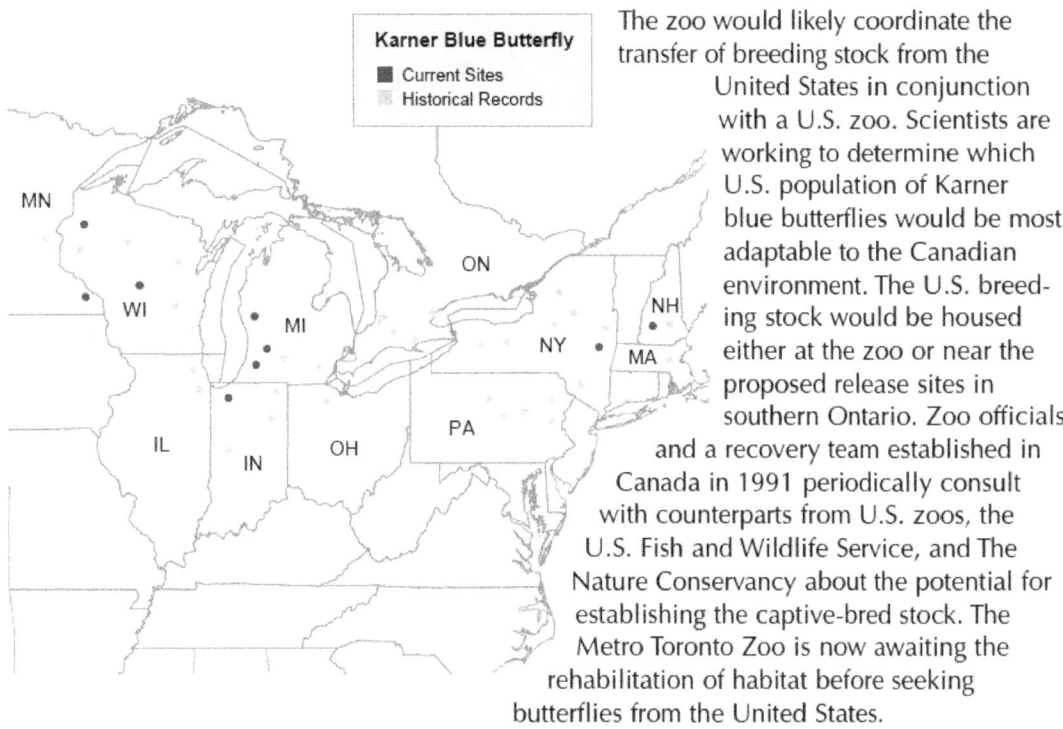

Karner Blue Butterfly
■ Current Sites
▨ Historical Records

The zoo would likely coordinate the transfer of breeding stock from the United States in conjunction with a U.S. zoo. Scientists are working to determine which U.S. population of Karner blue butterflies would be most adaptable to the Canadian environment. The U.S. breeding stock would be housed either at the zoo or near the proposed release sites in southern Ontario. Zoo officials and a recovery team established in Canada in 1991 periodically consult with counterparts from U.S. zoos, the U.S. Fish and Wildlife Service, and The Nature Conservancy about the potential for establishing the captive-bred stock. The Metro Toronto Zoo is now awaiting the rehabilitation of habitat before seeking butterflies from the United States.

For more than 10 years, the recovery team and other wildlife experts have worked to restore oak savannah at two select locations of former Karner blue butterfly habitat in southern Ontario. The restoration efforts include conducting controlled burns of vegetation, tree cutting, and planting of lupines and other plant species that the adult Karner blue butterfly feeds on for nectar. Biologists have also coordinated a program to reduce deer numbers, since deer grazing depleted much of the available butterfly habitat. The recovery of this habitat is focused on a holistic, community concept that will ideally see the revival of the whole range of flora and fauna indigenous to these two areas.

Another major cooperative effort was initiated in 1999, when the U.S. Fish and Wildlife Service, the Wisconsin Department of Natural Resources, and 25 partners (including utilities and conservation organizations) created a Habitat Conservation Plan to protect habitat for the butterflies across the State. These plans work with public and private landowners on small or large scales and can benefit other species as well.

Western Prairie Fringed Orchid
(Platanthera praeclara)

STATUS

Canada (COSEWIC): Endangered

U.S. (USFWS): Threatened

DESCRIPTION

The western prairie fringed orchid is a tall, erect, long-living perennial plant. The smooth stem grows to about 1 meter (about 3 feet) in height. The orchid grows two to five leaves that are thick and hairless. Each stalk produces an average of 20 large white to creamy flowers about 2.5 centimeters (1 inch) long. The lip, or lower petal, of each flower is deeply three-lobed and fringed. The sepals are tinged with pale green.

Donald Gunn

ECOLOGY

The western prairie fringed orchid occurs mostly in remnant native prairies and meadows, usually alone or in small groups. It emerges in late May and blooms in July. The flowers can last 10 days, and can be pollinated by only a few species of insects. Reproduction occurs by seed, with each seed capsule producing many thousands (perhaps millions) of tiny, wind- or water-dispersed seeds. For seedlings to become established, a specific fungus must be present in the soil that provides the plant with water and nutrients.

CAUSES OF DECLINE

Historically, the western prairie fringed orchid extended from Minnesota, Montana, and North Dakota south as far as Texas. Orchid numbers declined with the conversion of its tall-grass prairie habitat to cropland. They now occur mostly in southeastern Manitoba (where they were discovered in the 1980s), Minnesota, and North Dakota. In recent years, researchers have also discovered several populations in Nebraska. The number of flowering plants can fluctuate from year to year. The highest number observed in recent years in Manitoba was about 21,000 flowering plants, and about 15,000 flowering plants in the entire United States. The orchid occurs most often in wet, uncultivated prairie and meadows, but has been found in old fields and roadside ditches. Current threats include introduced invasive plants, filling of wetlands, intensive hay mowing, fire suppression, and overgrazing. Severe weather fluctuations, such as drought, flooding, and frost, as well as contact with herbicides used to control weeds also threaten the orchid.

In the late 1990s, scientists in Canada and the United States prepared separate recovery plans for the western prairie fringed orchid. The Canadian plan drew heavily from the American one. In 1999, Canadian and U.S. scientists established a western prairie fringed orchid working group. The group hopes to advance the recovery of this species across jurisdictional boundaries throughout its range. Primary working group goals include sharing information on the biology of the species, cooperating to improve management and stewardship, prioritizing recovery needs, and working together to obtain funding for recovery efforts. Initially, this group has focused on the northern part of the species' range, but also exchanges information with contacts in more southern states where the orchid occurs. About 80 percent of known orchid sites are protected in preserves or other publicly managed areas, mostly in Manitoba, Minnesota, and North Dakota. The group met in North Dakota in the summer of 1999 and Manitoba in the summer of 2000. Scientists made presentations on orchid research, management, and recovery efforts.

The working group is seeking funding to develop and implement a pilot program of "orchid friendly" management agreements with private landowners. Many orchid sites occur on private lands, where farmers or other landowners have maintained the species through conservation-minded agricultural practices. Biologists have launched an initial pilot project in North Dakota, and participating agencies are assisting in developing guidelines for grazing, burning, or weed control to maintain and/or enhance orchid habitat. In Manitoba, under a prairie management plan, the provincial government and several wildlife groups have also begun negotiating land purchases and conservation agreements with landowners. In Minnesota, wildlife officials are conducting periodic prescribed burning on most orchid preserves, which reduces mulch build-up and controls the increase of invasive grasses that can threaten the orchid. Grazing, which also reduces mulch, is permitted in some orchid preserves, such as in the Sheyenne National Grassland of North Dakota.

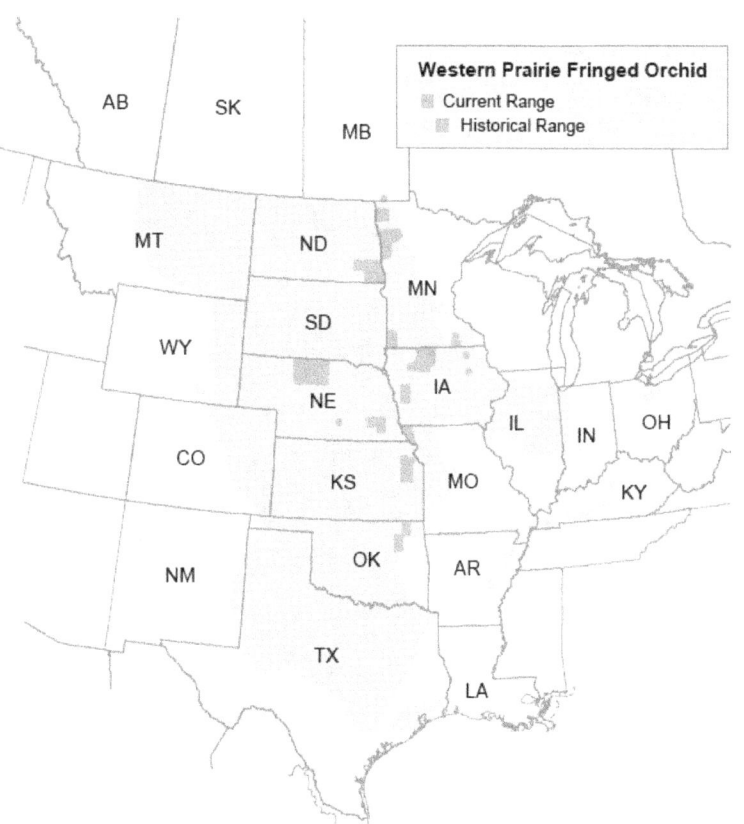

Western Prairie Fringed Orchid
- Current Range
- Historical Range

Shared Animal and Plant Species Federally Listed in the United States and/or Canada (Excluding Fish, Marine Mammals, Sea Turtles)

Common Name	Scientific Name	Federal Status - Canada [COSEWIC]	Federal Status - US [FWS]
Mammals			
Badger, American	Taxidea taxus jacksoni and T.t. jeffersonii	E	–
Bat, pallid	Antrozous pallidus	T	–
Bear, grizzly	Ursus arctos	XT-Prairie population SC-all others	T-Lower 48 states, XN
Bison, wood	Bison bison athabascae	T	E-Canada
Caribou, woodland	Rangifer tarandus caribou	E-Atlantic-Gaspésie population T-Boreal and Southern Mountain populations	E-Selkirk population
Cougar, eastern (eastern puma)	Puma concolor couguar Puma (=Felis)	E '97, DD '98	E
Ferret, black-footed	Mustela nigripes	XT	E, XN
Fox, swift	Vulpes velox	E	E-Canada population
Lynx, Canada	Lynx canadensis	–	T
Mole, Townsend's	Scapanus townsendii	T	–
Shrew, Pacific water	Sorex bendirii	T	–
Wolf, gray	Canis lupus	DD	E, T-Minnesota, XN
Wolverine	Gulo gulo	E-Eastern population	–
Birds			
Bobwhite, northern	Colinus virginianus	E	–
Chat, yellow-breasted	Icteria virens auricollis	E-British Columbia population	–
Crane, whooping	Grus americana	E	E, XN
Curlew, eskimo	Numenius borealis	E	E
Duck, harlequin	Histrionicus histrionicus	E-Eastern population	–
Eagle, bald	Haliaeetus leucocephalus	–	T
Falcon, anatum peregrine	Falco peregrinus anatum	T	–
Flycatcher, Acadian	Empidonax virescens	E	–
Goshawk, Queen Charlotte	Accipiter gentilis laingi	T	–
Grouse, sage	Centrocercus urophasianus urophasianus	E-Prairie population	–
Murrelet, marbled	Brachyramphus marmoratus	T	T-California, Oregon, Washington
Owl, barn	Tyto alba	E-Eastern population	–
Owl, burrowing	Speotyto cunicularia	E	–
Owl, northern spotted	Strix occidentalis caurina	E	T
Pelican, California brown	Pelecanus occidentalis californicus	–	E-Pacific coast, western Gulf of Mexico
Pipit, Sprague's	Anthus spragueii	T	–
Plover, mountain	Charadrius montanus	E	PT
Plover, piping	Charadrius melodus	E	E-Great Lakes population T-Atlantic Coast and Northern Great Plains populations
Prairie-chicken, greater	Tympanuchus cupido	XT	–
Rail, king	Rallus elegans	E	–
Shrike, loggerhead	Lanius ludovicianus migrans	E-Eastern population	–
Shrike, loggerhead	Lanius ludovicianus excubitorides	T-Prairie population	–
Sparrow, Henslow's	Ammodramus henslowii	E	–
Tern, roseate	Sterna dougallii	E	E-Atlantic Coast population T-except Atlantic Coast population
Thrasher, sage	Oreoscoptes montanus	E	–
Warbler, hooded	Wilsonia citrina	T	–
Warbler, Kirtland's	Dendroica kirtlandii	E	E
Warbler, prothonotary	Protonotaria citrea	E	–
Woodpecker, white-headed	Picoides albolarvatus	E	–
Reptiles			
Lizard, pygmy short-horned	Phrynosoma douglassii douglassii	XT-British Columbia population	–
Rattlesnake, eastern Massasauga	Sistrurus catenatus catenatus	T	–
Snake, black rat	Elaphe obsoleta obsoleta	T	–
Snake, blue racer	Coluber constrictor foxii	E	–
Snake, eastern fox	Elaphe vulpina gloydi	T	–
Snake, Lake Erie water	Nerodia sipedon insularum	E	T
Snake, queen	Regina septemvittata	T	–
Snake, sharp-tailed	Contia tenuis	E	–
Turtle, spiny softshell	Apalone spinifera	T	–
Amphibians			
Frog, northern cricket	Acris crepitans	E	–
Frog, northern leopard	Rana pipiens	E-Southern Mountain population	–
Frog, Oregon spotted	Rana pretiosa	E	–
Salamander, Jefferson	Ambystoma jeffersonianum	T	–
Salamander, Pacific giant	Dicamptodon tenebrosus	T	–
Toad, Fowler's	Bufo fowleri (B. woodhousii fowleri)	T	–
Molluscs			
Bean, rayed	Villosa fabalis	E	–
Lampmussel, wavy-rayed	Lampsilis fasciola	E	–
Riffleshell, northern	Epioblasma torulosa rangiana	E	E
Wedgemussel, dwarf	Alasmidonta heterodon	XT	E

Common Name	Scientific Name	Federal Status - Canada [COSEWIC]	Federal Status - US [FWS]
Insects			
Beetle, American burying (=giant carrion)	Nicrophorus americanus	–	E
Beetle, Hungerford's crawling water	Brychius hungerfordi	–	E
Butterfly, Karner blue	Lycaeides melissa samuelis	XT	E
Checkerspot, Taylor's	Euphydryas editha taylori	E	–
Hairstreak, Behr's (Columbia)	Satyrium behrii columbia	T	–
Skipper, Dun	Euphyes vestris	T-Western population	–
Plants [sorted alphabetically by Scientific Name]			
Verbena, sand	Abronia micrantha	T	–
Fern, southern maidenhair	Adiantum capillus-veneris	E	–
Agalinis, Gattinger's	Agalinis gattingeri	E	–
Agalinis, Skinner's	Agalinis skinneriana	E	–
Colicroot	Aletris farinosa	T	–
Ammannia, scarlet	Ammannia robusta	E	–
Fern, American hart's-tongue	Asplenium Scolopendrium americanum	–	T
Aster, Anticosti	Aster anticostensis	T	–
Aster, white-top	Aster curtus	T	–
Aster, white wood	Aster divaricatus	T	–
Fern, Mexican mosquito	Azolla mexicana	T	–
Balsamroot, deltoid	Balsamorhiza deltoidea	E	–
Moss, apple	Bartramia stricta	E	–
Bluehearts	Buchnera americana	E	–
Sedge, juniper	Carex juniperorum	E	–
Sedge, false hop	Carex lupuliformis	E	–
Chestnut, American	Castanea dentata	T	–
Paintbrush, golden	Castilleja levisecta	E	T
Orchid, phantom	Cephalanthera austiniae	T	–
Wintergreen, spotted	Chimaphila maculata	E	–
Thistle, Pitcher's or dune	Cirsium pitcheri	E	T
Pepperbush, sweet	Clethra alnifolia	T	–
Blue-eyed Mary	Collinsia verna	XT	–
Coreopsis, Pink	Coreopsis rosea	E	–
Cryptanthe, tiny	Cryptantha minima	E	–
Lady's-slipper, small white	Cypripedium candidum	E	–
Prairie-clover, hairy	Dalea villosa var. villosa	T	–
Tick-trefoil, Illinois	Desmodium illinoense	XT	–
Sundew, thread-leaved	Drosera filiformis	E	–
Spike-rush, horsetail	Eleocharis equisetoides	E	–
Gentian, white prairie	Gentiana alba	E	–
Avens, Eastern Mountain	Geum peckii	E	–
Coffee-tree, Kentucky	Gymnocladus dioicus	T	–
Mouse-ear-cress, slender	Halimolobos virgata	T	–
Goldenseal	Hydrastis canadensis	T	–
Water-pennywort	Hydrocotyle umbellata	T	–

Common Name	Scientific Name	Federal Status - Canada [COSEWIC]	Federal Status - US [FWS]
Daisy, lakeside	Hymenoxys herbacea (=acaulis var. glabra)	–	T
Iris, dwarf lake	Iris lacustris	–	T
Blue-flag, Western	Iris missouriensis	T	–
Quillwort, Engelmann's	Isoetes engelmannii	E	–
Pogonia, small whorled	Isotria medeoloides	E	T
Pogonia, large whorled	Isotria verticillata	E	–
Water-willow, American	Justicia americana	T	–
Redroot	Lachnanthes caroliana	T	–
Bush-clover, slender	Lespedeza virginica	E	–
Twayblade, purple	Liparis liliifolia	E	–
Lipocarpha, small-flowered	Lipocarpha micrantha	T	–
Golden crest	Lophiola aurea	T	–
Lotus, seaside birds-foot	Lotus formosissimus	E	–
Lupine, prairie	Lupinus lepidus var. lepidus	E	–
Tree, cucumber	Magnolia acuminata	E	–
Mulberry, red	Morus rubra	E	–
Cactus, eastern prickly pear	Opuntia humifusa	E	–
Ginseng, American	Panax quinquefolium	E	–
Lousewort, Furbish's	Pedicularis furbishiae	E	E
Plantain, heart-leaved	Plantago cordata	E	–
Orchid, eastern prairie fringed	Platanthera leucophaea	SC	T
Orchid, western prairie fringed	Platanthera praeclara	E	T
Jacob's Ladder, van Brunt's	Polemonium van-bruntiae	T	–
Milkwort, pink	Polygala incarnata	E	–
Mountain-mint, hoary	Pycnanthemum incanum	E	–
Buttercup, water-plantain	Ramunculus alismaefolius var. alismaefolius	E	–
Toothcup	Rotala ramosior	E	–
Gentian, plymouth	Sabatia kennedyana	T	–
Greenbrier, round-leaved [Ontario population]	Smilax rotundifolia	T	–
Goldenrod, Houghton's	Solidago houghtonii	–	T
Wood-poppy	Stylophorum diphyllum	E	–
Aster, western silver-leaved	Symphyotrichum sericeum	T	–
Goat's-rue, Virginia	Tephrosia virginiana	E	–
Spiderwort, western	Tradescantia occidentalis	T	–
Bulrush, bashful	Trichophorum planifolium	E	–
Trillium, drooping	Trillium flexipes	E	–
Pogonia, nodding	Triphora trianthophora	E	–
Owl-clover, bearded	Triphysaria versicolor ssp. versicolor	E	–
Soapweed	Yucca glauca	T	–
Deerberry	Vaccinium stamineum	T	–
Violet, bird's-foot	Viola pedata	T	–
Violet, yellow montane	Viola praemorsa ssp. praemorsa	T	–
Woodsia, blunt-lobed	Woodsia obtusa	E	–

Sources: U.S. List (50 CFR 17.11 17.12), COSEWIC List (2000).

United States

Endangered (E)
Any species which is in danger of extinction throughout all or a significant portion of its range other than a species of the Class Insecta determined by the Secretary to constitute a pest whose protection under the provisions of this Act would present an overwhelming and overriding risk to man.

Threatened (T)
Any species which is likely to become an endangered species within the foreseeable future throughout all or a significant portion of its range.

Experimental Population (XN)
A population of a listed species re-established outside its current range but within the probable historical range.

Proposed Threatened (PT)
Proposed to be listed as threatened.

Note: The U S. list is updated continually and includes foreign countries.

Canada

Extirpated (XT)
A wildlife species that no longer exists in the wild in Canada, but exists elsewhere in the wild.

Endangered (E)
A wildlife species that is facing imminent extirpation or extinction.

Threatened (T)
A wildlife species that is likely to become endangered if limiting factors are not reversed.

Special Concern (SC)
A wildlife species is of special concern because of characteristics that make it particularly sensitive to human activities or natural events.

Data Deficient (DD)
A wildlife species for which there is insufficient scientific information to support status designation.

Note: The Canadian list is updated bi-annually and does not include foreign countries.

What You Can Do

Under the U.S.-Canada Framework, any interested party, whether government or private, may seek the assistance of either of the two Federal wildlife agencies in establishing cooperative programs with its counterpart in the other country, even if the species is at risk in only one of the two countries. Here are some things the public can do to help protect wild species:

- Report sightings of migratory species, like whooping cranes, to area wildlife agencies. Scientists carefully monitor species during migration to determine what flight paths they are following, where their staging grounds are along the way, and what influences are impacting on them during the journey;

- Observe the behavior of species at risk and let biologists know what you've learned. Keen naturalists in California were the first to observe that marbled murrelets feed at dawn and dusk, critical information in efforts to protect this small bird;

- Cooperate with scientists in research and recovery activities. Hundreds of volunteers have participated in international piping plover inventories, helping officials to identify plover numbers and habitat in the wild;

- Join local wildlife groups. Many conservation organizations have local chapters, and, in many rural and urban areas, groups have been established to help preserve specific species or groups of species or restore their habitats;

- Inform area wildlife agencies of opportunities for developing or expanding endangered species recovery cooperation. You may live near the habitat of an endangered species that no one knows about, or know of ways the habitat of a known species could be enhanced or protected;

- Do not disrupt the habitat of a species at risk. For the piping plover, for example, biologists ask the public to respect all areas fenced or posted as plover habitat, to not approach or linger near plover nests, to keep pets on a leash and cats indoors, and to refrain from littering beaches, which attracts plover predators like raccoons;

- Ensure that species at risk are not in harm's way. For example, biologists helping to recover the Lake Erie water snake suggest that you use a broom, rake, or stick to gently encourage this harmless, nonvenomous species to move off roads and away from boat motors and other machinery where they can be injured.

- Learn about species at risk, and tell others what you have learned, at home, in conversation, during trips into the wild, or at school. Many wildlife agencies give out brochures, posters, videos, or other communications materials that describe a species at risk and explain how its decline contributes to reducing the planet's cherished plant and animal diversity.

- Respect endangered species laws. In the United States, the Endangered Species Act carries protective measures for listed species. For example, it is illegal to remove or destroy any western prairie fringed orchids in any area under Federal jurisdiction, or to knowingly violate any State law protecting the species. In Canada, several Provinces have laws that protect species at risk. As well, an Accord for the Protection of Species at Risk has been approved-in-principle by Federal, Provincial, and Territorial wildlife ministers. Other pieces of Federal and Provincial legislation, such as the Migratory Bird Convention Act, also afford protection to species at risk.

- Protect natural areas from invasive species. Plant only species that are native to your area for landscaping and habitat restoration. Do not release any animals into the wild that didn't come from that location.

FOR MORE INFORMATION

In Canada, contact the Canadian Wildlife Service at 1-800-668-6767 or visit [www.speciesatrisk.gc.ca]. In the United States, contact the U.S. Fish and Wildlife Service at 1-800-344-WILD or visit [http://endangered.fws.gov].

This publication is also available in French and online at either web site.

Framework for Cooperation Between the U.S. Department of the Interior and Environment Canada in the Protection and Recovery of Wild Species at Risk

The goal of this framework is to prevent populations of wild species shared by the United States and Canada from becoming extinct as a consequence of human activity, through the conservation of wildlife populations and the ecosystems on which they depend.

THE UNITED STATES AND CANADA:

- share a common concern for and commitment to the protection and recovery of wild species at risk of extinction;
- have a long history of cooperation in the management of shared populations of wildlife and plants, as demonstrated by collaborative efforts for the recovery of endangered migratory species such as the whooping crane *(Grus americana)* and the piping plover *(Charadrius melodus)*;
- recognize that greater success in protecting and recovering shared populations of species at risk can be achieved through cooperative, coordinated action; and
- acknowledge that conservation action is most often effective when implemented using a multi-species approach at the landscape level.

THE UNITED STATES DEPARTMENT OF THE INTERIOR AND ENVIRONMENT CANADA ANNOUNCE A FRAMEWORK FOR COOOPERATIVE ACTION TO:

i. facilitate the exchange of information and technical expertise regarding the conservation of species at risk and their habitat;

ii. harmonize the evaluation and identification of such species;

iii. provide a means of identifying species at risk that require bilateral action;

iv. promote the development and implementation of joint or multi-national recovery plans for species identified as endangered or threatened;

v. encourage expanded and more effective partnerships between our two agencies and states, provinces, and territorial aboriginal and tribal governments, and the private sector (individuals, conservation groups, corporations, etc.) in recovery efforts;

vi. create greater public awareness and involvement regarding the need to conserve wildlife populations and the ecosystems on which they depend, and to prevent the loss of shared species; and

vii. use the cooperative arrangements established in the Trilateral Committee for Wildlife and Ecosystem Conservation and Management to provide a mechanism for establishing mutual priorities, coordinating recovery actions, and ensuring efficient use of available resources for the protection and recovery of species at risk.

The implementing agencies for this framework are the U.S. Fish and Wildlife Service of the U.S. Department of the Interior and the Canadian Wildlife Service of Environment Canada.

In recognition of the continental nature and importance of many species at risk, and existing partnerships, the United States and Canada intend to invite the participation of Mexico in this framework.

Signed at Washington, D.C.
This 7th day of April 1997;

For the United States of America
Department of the Interior

For Canada
Department of the Environment

Secretary Bruce Babbitt

Minister Sergio Marchi

Credits

Canada

Reviewers of maps and text:

B.C. Ministry of Environment, Lands, and Parks: Matt Austen, Ian Hatter, James Quayle

Canadian Wildlife Service: Diane Amirault, Theresa Anískowicz-Fowler, Lu Carbyn, Paul Goossen, Brian Johns, Ken Morgan, Simon Nadeau, Kent Prior

Manitoba Conservation: Jason Greenall

Ontario Ministry of Natural Resources: Terry Crabe, Mike Oldham

Saskatchewan Environment and Resource Management: Earl Wiltse

Canadian coordinator: Danielle Gagnon, Canadian Wildlife Service

Text: West Hawk Associates Inc.

Maps: Mike Elliot, Canadian Wildlife Service

Design: ACR Communications Inc.

United States

Reviewers of maps and text:

Oklahoma Department of Wildlife Conservation: Julianne Hoagland

U.S. Fish and Wildlife Service: Suzanne Audet, Anne Hecht, Buddy Fazio, Lee Folliard, Pete Gober, Karen Kreil, Mike Lockhart, Bob Murphy, Robyn Niver, Christopher Servheen, Janet Smith, Tom Stehn

U.S. Geological Survey: Marsha Sovada

University of Minnesota: Jennifer Stucker

U.S. coordinator: Susan Jewell, U.S. Fish and Wildlife Service

 Environment Canada

Environnement Canada

Canadian Wildlife Service

Service canadien de la faune

U.S. Department of he Interior
Fish and Wildlife Service